A Party for Puppies

by Anne O'Brien
illustrated by Olivia Cole

Core Decodable 73

McGraw Hill Education

Bothell, WA • Chicago, IL • Columbus, OH • New York, NY

MHEonline.com

Send all inquiries to:
McGraw-Hill Education
8787 Orion Place
Columbus, OH 43240

ISBN: 978-0-02-143357-5
MHID: 0-02-143357-7

Printed in the United States of America.

9 10 11 12 KOD 24

Nellie and Billy have fun parties.
They invite Nellie's babies and teddies.

Nellie gets a table. Billy sets the table.
Every puppy helps.

Nellie makes funny party hats.
Billy tapes ribbons on every hat.

Nellie has garden treats.
Billy places a treat on every plate.
Every puppy helps.

Nellie gets more yummy treats.
"No more help, please!" yells Nellie.

The party is over.

Happy puppies help clean up.

"Thanks for the help," Billy mutters.